science

Electricity

Angela Royston

WAYLAND

Explore the world with **Popcorn** - your complete first non-fiction library.

Look out for more titles in the **Popcorn** range. All books have the same format of simple text and vibrant images. Text is carefully matched to the pictures to help readers to identify and understand key vocabulary.
www.waylandbooks.co.uk/popcorn

Wayland Australia
Level 17/207 Kent Street
Sydney NSW 2000

Editor: Katie Powell
Designer: Robert Walster
Picture Researcher: Diana Morris

British Library Cataloguing in Publication Data
Royston, Angela.
  Electricity. -- (Popcorn. Science corner)
  1. Electricity--Juvenile literature.
  I. Title II. Series
  537-dc22
ISBN: 978 0 7502 6438 9

Printed and bound in China

Wayland is a division of Hachette Children's Books,
an Hachette UK Company
www.hachette.co.uk

Photographs:
Leslie Garland/Alamy: 13.
Wayne Howard/stockphoto: 8.
Inner Shadows/istockphoto: 12
Brad Killer/istockphoto: 4.
Sean Locke/istockphoto: 6.
John Carne Molla/Corbis: 1, 10.
Photogenes: 11.
Kevin Russ/istockphoto: 9.
Jon Schulte/istockphoto: 2, 7.
Raul Touzon/National Geographic/Getty
Images: front cover.
Tony Tremblay /istockphoto: 5.
Wayland: 14, 15, 16, 17, 18, 19, 20, 21, 22, 23.

Contents

What is electricity?

Electricity is used to make things work. When electricity flows through an electrical machine it makes the machine work.

A fridge uses electricity to keep food cold.

You cannot see electricity but you can see what it does. Electricity can be very powerful. It is even strong enough to move trains.

electric wires

Warning! Electricity can be dangerous. An electric shock can kill you.

This train takes electricity from the wires above it.

Using electricity

People use electricity in their homes. A television set makes sounds and pictures when electricity flows through it.

We use electricity to make light at night. A bulb lights up when electricity flows through it.

Electrical machines

A kitchen often has several machines that need electricity to work. A microwave oven, and a fridge both work using electricity.

Can you see which machines in this kitchen need electricity to work?

Electricity can make things hot.
For example, an electric iron
gets very hot.

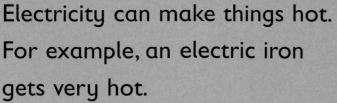

Warning!
An electric iron
stays hot for
a while after
it has been
turned off.

9

Where does electricity come from?

Electricity is made in power stations. Thick cables carry electricity away from the power station. They take it to cities and towns.

As water flows through this dam, it makes electricity.

The cables are linked to thinner wires. Electricity flows through these wires to different buildings.

cable

In towns and cities, some electric cables and wires are hidden under the ground.

Sockets and plugs

Wires bring electricity into your home.
Electric sockets connect to the wires.
When a machine is plugged into a socket,
electricity flows through the machine.

Warning!
Do not put
anything into an
electric socket
except a plug
that fits it.

Some wires lead to electric lights.
You push the switch to make the
electricity flow. Then the light
comes on!

Batteries

A battery gives a small amount of electricity.
Batteries are so small they can fit into
objects, such as a toy car or a torch.
This makes them easy to carry around.

This toy car runs
on a battery that
fits into the back
of the car.

Some batteries are round and some are square. You have to use the battery that fits the toy or machine.

This remote control uses two AA batteries.

A simple circuit

A simple circuit uses electricity from a battery. A circuit is a path that allows electricity to flow all the way around it.

As electricity passes through the bulb, the bulb lights up.

wire

bulb

battery case

A simple circuit can have a buzzer
instead of a bulb. As electricity passes
through the buzzer in this circuit,
the buzzer makes a noise.

buzzer

battery case

Making a circuit

You can make a simple circuit with a battery, a bulb and two wires. Use the wires to join the battery to the bulb.

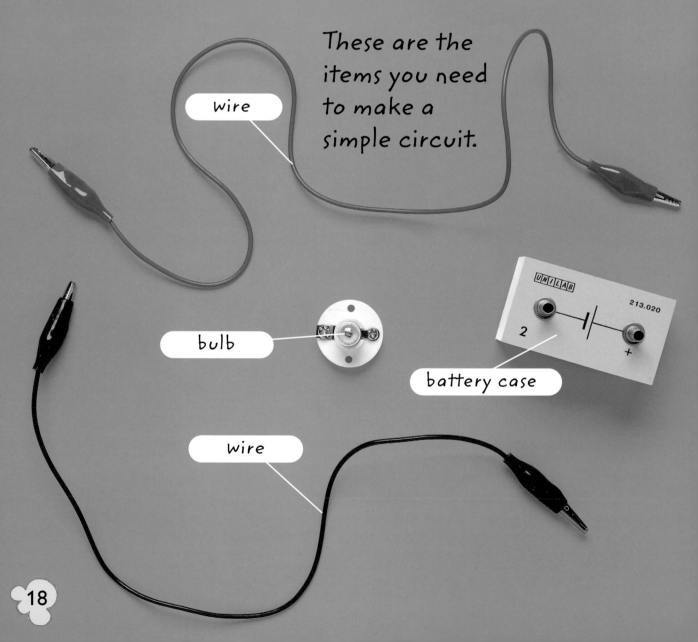

These are the items you need to make a simple circuit.

wire

bulb

battery case

wire

UNILAB

213.020

2

+

If the circuit is not connected correctly, the electricity will not flow. One of the wires in this circuit is not attached to the bulb, so the bulb will not light up.

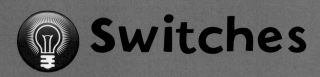

Switches

A switch opens and closes a circuit. When the switch is closed, electricity flows around the circuit. The bulb lights up.

Every electrical machine has a switch to turn it on and off.

bulb

switch

battery case

When the switch is open, electricity cannot flow around the circuit. The bulb goes off.

Make your own switch

You will need:
- a battery
- a bulb
- two wires
- a paper clip

Follow these simple steps to make a switch.

1. Set up a simple circuit using a battery, a bulb and two wires.

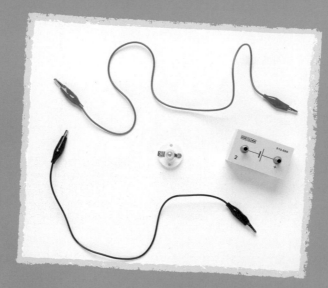

2. Undo one of the wires to the bulb. What happens?

3. Attach the end of the wire to a paper clip.

4. Now touch the screw on the bulb with the paper clip. What happens?

You have a made a switch!

23

Glossary

battery a sealed packet of chemicals that make electricity

cable a thick rope of wires

circuit an unbroken path that electricity can flow around

electricity a form of energy that is used to work electrical machines

power station a building in which electricity is made

socket a set of holes which link a plug to wires carrying electricity

switch a device for turning the flow of electricity on and off

Index